Look Inside You

a selection of poetry

by

L . D Stranack

other titles by L.D Stranack

3 am Thoughts

The Sunsets of My Mind

Forever In Bloom

Acknowledgements

For my parents.
Thank you for your constant encouragement
and love.

I Love You

LOOK INSIDE YOU

LOOK INSIDE YOU

A photographic book of poems covering topics we are all too familiar with. I hope to motivate and inspire you whilst providing comfort and hope in this sometimes, cold world.

From my heart to yours.

- LS

LOOK INSIDE YOU

CONTENTS

1 Mental Health —————————— pages 1-13

2 Love ———————————————— pages 14-27

3 Grief ———————————————— pages 28-42

4 Self Care ————————————— pages 43-52

5 Heartbreak ————————————— pages 53-63

6 Healing ————————————————— pages 64-77

7 Joy ——————————————————— pages 65-98

LOOK INSIDE YOU

MENTAL HEALTH

LOOK INSIDE YOU

LOOK INSIDE YOU

And there are those days when
the numbness silently invades,
and all you yearn for is solitude.
Isolation and detachment are
your only allies.
And this numbness washes over you like a
black murky wave of nothingness,
and even though you try your hardest
to fight against it, you have
absolutely no resolve.
You're helpless, you surrender, you allow it to
drag you under, you don't want to breathe.
You silently give it permission to
slowly drown you.
And yet somehow, you're okay with that.
And how long it will stay, you have no idea.
But eventually at some point it will diminish.
And you'll muster the strength to rise
up and fill your lungs with air,
to finally breathe.
And you'll swim back to the shore.
You'll swim back to who you were
and the life before.

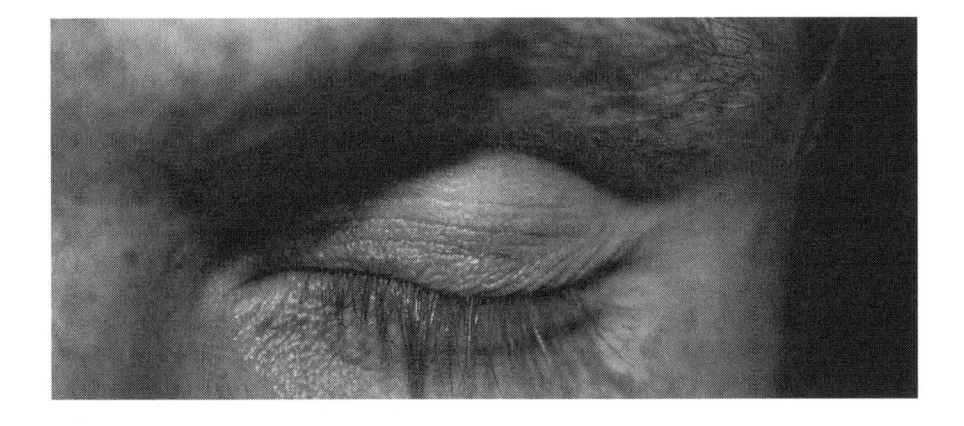

LOOK INSIDE YOU

You see me.
Even when I
hide from the rest of
the world.
You hear me.
Even when I am silent.
You feel me.
Even on the days
I am not there.

/LS

LOOK INSIDE YOU

I have become exceptionally
good at hiding.
When I hide I am safe.
I am anonymous.
I am not open to judgement.
I can retreat into the shadows
of my own mind.
And there I will bide my time,
until I am ready to be whole again.

/LS

LOOK INSIDE YOU

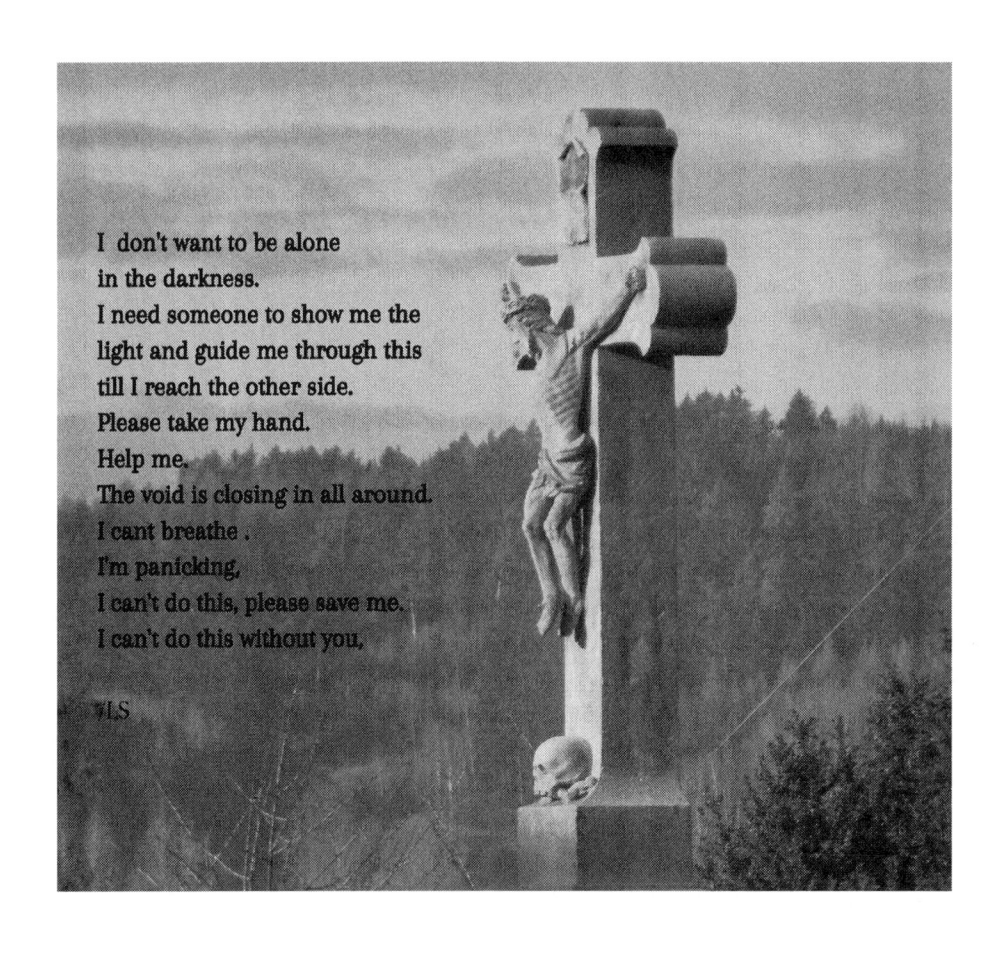

I don't want to be alone
in the darkness.
I need someone to show me the
light and guide me through this
till I reach the other side.
Please take my hand.
Help me.
The void is closing in all around.
I cant breathe .
I'm panicking,
I can't do this, please save me.
I can't do this without you,

JLS

LOOK INSIDE YOU

And as I lay there on my bed,
I was aware of my heartbeat,
for the first time in a long time.
And I realised there and then
how the majority of the time
I live in my head,
and how little I live in my body.

/LS

LOOK INSIDE YOU

It is perfectly acceptable to
cut off people who
compromise your mental health.
And the more you put you first
the more people you'll lose.
It's a given rule.
You're not stuck.
You have choices.
You can think new thoughts.
You can break old patterns.
Decide today that *you* come first,
and never look back.
That burden you've unloaded
wasn't yours to carry.

/LS

LOOK INSIDE YOU

I'm done with crying a river.
I've decided I'll become one instead.
I will flow where I choose,
and deepen where I settle.
I'll cascade down mountains,
and flow into the sea.
There will be no more tears,
I will surely be free.

/LS

LOOK INSIDE YOU

True bravery is not putting
on a false face and trying to
hide your injured soul,
or disguising your fragmented heart
from the world,
trying to pretend that
everything is okay.
No, it is sitting on the floor
with your head in your hands,
crying your heart out
and feeling every bit of your
gut wrenching pain.
That's a warrior.
That is bravery.

/LS

LOOK INSIDE YOU

I have two reasons why I'm afraid
of letting people in.
The darkness they may bring,
and the darkness they may find,
in those murky corners of my mind.

/LS

LOOK INSIDE YOU

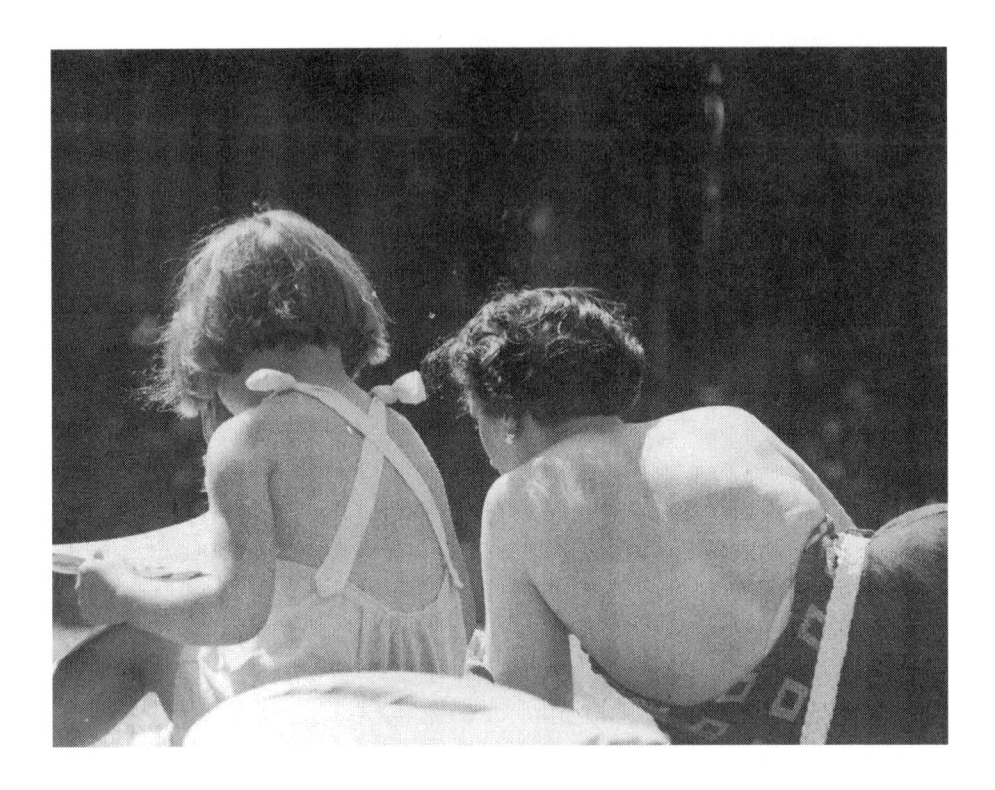

Some days I let the phone ring.
I don't feel like showering.
I retreat into my head.
I'll play songs on repeat.
I'll chew my fingers till they bleed.
I'll sleep so I don't need to feel.
And do you know what?
Every single one of those
things are justifiable.
We all have coping mechanisms.
We are all uniquely arranged.
We deal with our darknesses differently.
But we are no less human for it.

/LS

LOOK INSIDE YOU

To anyone who has ever been
told they're *"too much"*.
If only you knew how your
"too much" one day could
make people feel more than *enough*.

/LS

LOOK INSIDE YOU

LOOK INSIDE YOU

LOVE

LOOK INSIDE YOU

LOOK INSIDE YOU

Some people don't say
"I love you" like most people.
They say things like;
Have you eaten today?
iI saw this and thought of you
Text me when you get there.

Listen carefully.

/LS

LOOK INSIDE YOU

And then one night they stopped
chasing the moon,
and they shone brighter
than the sun.
They stopped reaching for the stars,
and their love became one.
It shone the brightest in the sky.
The light that would never go out.
Their love was divine,
beyond immeasurable doubt.

/LS

LOOK INSIDE YOU

I have no desire to compete for your love.
If you must choose between me
and another then choose them.
I won't settle for being an option.
I belong on a golden pedestal
with diamonds at my feet.
And I won't settle for less
than that.

/LS

LOOK INSIDE YOU

Fall in love with someone who
will cherish your heart
and protect it from harm.
Someone who lays their soul
bare and doesn't harbour any dark secrets.
Someone who will move mountains
to be in your presence.
Who won't ever think of leaving your side.
That's a love worth having.

LS

LOOK INSIDE YOU

Take me completely.
Devour my body.
Invade my fantasies.
Ravage my lips till they
become numb.
I want to surrender all of it,
it's yours.
Lay me down and consume me.
I am an offering to you.

/LS

LOOK INSIDE YOU

Love never bothered me.
It was the desire i craved.
That I was an element of excitement
they would take the risk for.
Someone who craved my passion, my touch,
my aggression.
Love is okay.
But desire is what sets
my soul on fire.

/LS

LOOK INSIDE YOU

You're like a shot of vodka.
The taste of you sets my senses on fire.
You intoxicate me,
I need shot after shot.
I have to finish the whole bottle.
But oh, that rush.

/LS

LOOK INSIDE YOU

There are nights when I see you
in my dreams.
Here I patiently sit under our favourite tree.
The stars tell me you are coming,
and you appear beside me.
The sudden apparition of you makes me realise
just how much I crave you in the dream world and the physical.
I'm eternally tied to you by a silken thread.

/LS

LOOK INSIDE YOU

> Every love has it's time,
> This time just wasn't ours.
> But that doesn't mean it was
> never love.
> It just means it didn't belong
> here right now.
> It will belong somewhere in another time,
> of that I can assure you.

LOOK INSIDE YOU

When two people are in love
but are completely different,
that doesn't mean it can't go in their favour.
It's like the story of the rose and the thorns.
They can exist together
and live a beautiful life.
They compliment each other.
But without the contrast of the sharp and the fragile,
their love would be mediocre.

/LS

LOOK INSIDE YOU

And now that you
don't have to be perfect,
you can allow yourself
to be loved.
Let someone bask
in your existence,
adoring all the flaws
you claim you have.
For these are the traits
that soften your edges
and make you endearing.
Allow someone to worship
you under the moon.
you are beautiful
and rare.
You are poetry.

/LS

LOOK INSIDE YOU

LOOK INSIDE YOU

GRIEF

LOOK INSIDE YOU

Your loss burns a
cavity in my chest.
A constant flame
that never burns out.
And from that cavity,
the light escapes.
The light that is
my life.

/LS

LOOK INSIDE YOU

I see your face in the clouds.
I hear your whispers on the wind.
I smell your scent where your clothes now hang.
I taste you in the wine we once shared.
I reach out for you when I am asleep,
and I expect you to be there.
You seep into my bones, you are everywhere.
Your soul still lingers,
I can smell you in my hair.
I constantly grieve but my heart
is granted a reprieve,
for I know I am not alone
you are always beside me.

/LS

LOOK INSIDE YOU

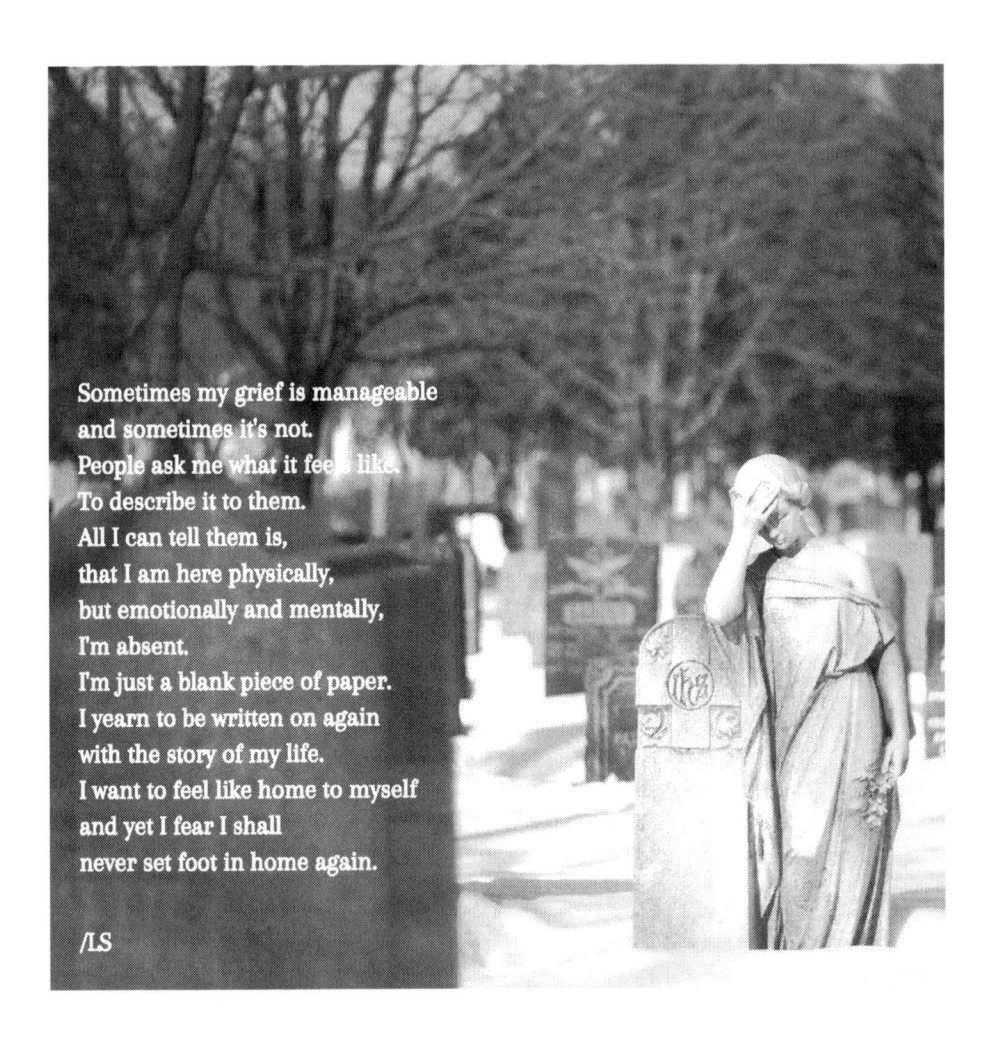

Sometimes my grief is manageable
and sometimes it's not.
People ask me what it feels like.
To describe it to them.
All I can tell them is,
that I am here physically,
but emotionally and mentally,
I'm absent.
I'm just a blank piece of paper.
I yearn to be written on again
with the story of my life.
I want to feel like home to myself
and yet I fear I shall
never set foot in home again.

/LS

LOOK INSIDE YOU

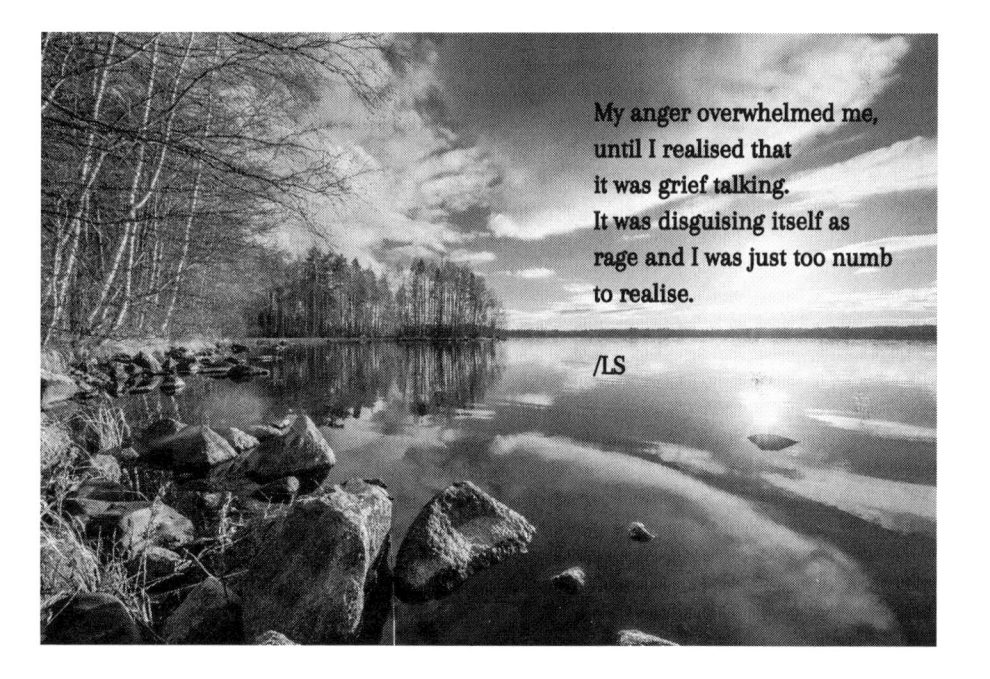

My anger overwhelmed me,
until I realised that
it was grief talking.
It was disguising itself as
rage and I was just too numb
to realise.

/LS

LOOK INSIDE YOU

Grief is just love
that has nowhere
left to go.
It's the love you want
to give but you can't.
It clings to places in you.
The heart.
The soul.
The pit of your stomach.
Behind your eyes.
That lump in your throat.
That is where it lingers.
It can never be felt
by the presence of you now.
Our love will never die,
it rests in peace in me forever.

/LS

LOOK INSIDE YOU

It is in that moment
just after waking,
before I realise where I am,
that it hits me.
That a part of me is gone.
The void encompasses me,
it feels like never
being able to feel
the sun on my face.
I yearn to bask
in the glow of it again.

/LS

LOOK INSIDE YOU

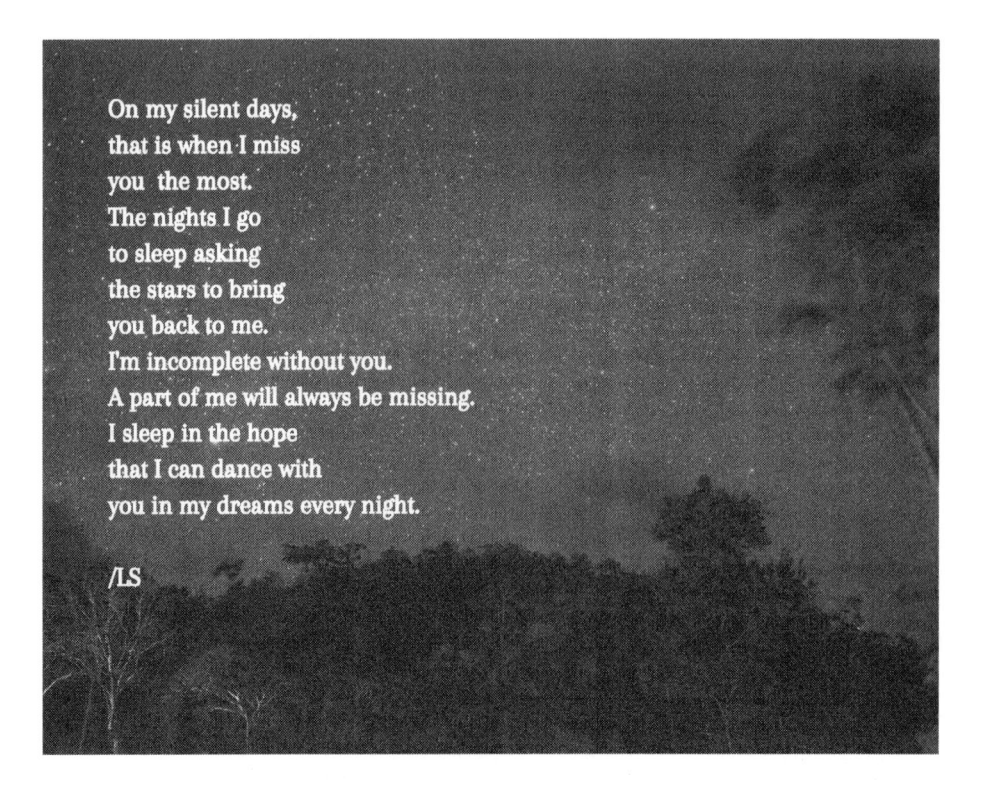

On my silent days,
that is when I miss
you the most.
The nights I go
to sleep asking
the stars to bring
you back to me.
I'm incomplete without you.
A part of me will always be missing.
I sleep in the hope
that I can dance with
you in my dreams every night.

/LS

LOOK INSIDE YOU

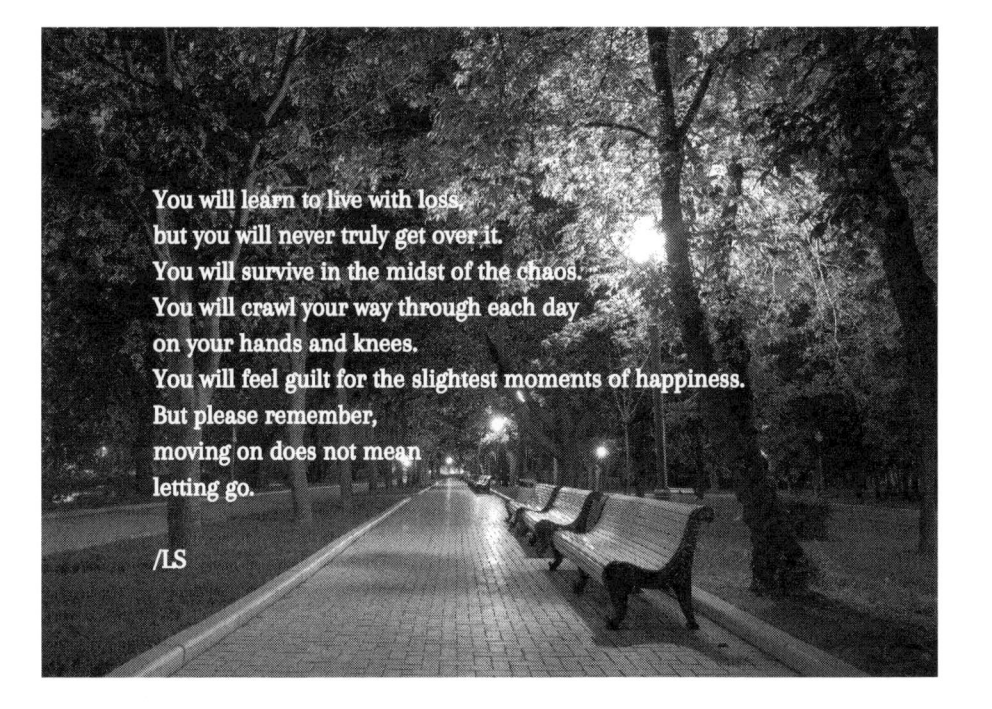

You will learn to live with loss,
but you will never truly get over it.
You will survive in the midst of the chaos.
You will crawl your way through each day
on your hands and knees.
You will feel guilt for the slightest moments of happiness.
But please remember,
moving on does not mean
letting go.

/LS

LOOK INSIDE YOU

This is not over.
It doesn't end here.
The veil of death
won't obscure our memories,
or our love.
Our story is a part of everything
that was and will ever be.
And eventually time will pass
in the blink of an eye,
and you'll be there
to greet me.
I'll look into your eyes,
I'll blow a kiss in the wind
and bid the earth goodbye,
we will start a new adventure
Together we will fly.

/LS

LOOK INSIDE YOU

Losing you has almost
destroyed me.
Gone is the person I was then.
I am replaced by a stranger
with an overwhelming sense
of hollowness.
I lack my own identity.
I am drowning in desolation.
My heart has been ripped from my chest.
I will never be who I was before
and that is also something I grieve.
The loss of
ME.

/LS

LOOK INSIDE YOU

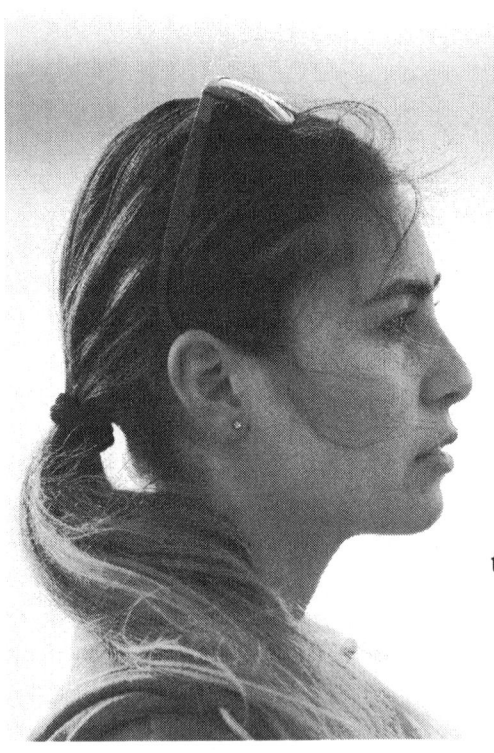

Listen to the silence.
It hangs in the air like static.
A pure white noise.
I have often wished I could
see it with my own eyes.
The vacuum that holds so
many unseen things.
My sadness hangs in it,
the deafening silence envelops me.
If I open a window
will it escape?

/LS

LOOK INSIDE YOU

Why do we think it is heroic to suffer in silence? Silence can be a crippling affliction.

/LS

LOOK INSIDE YOU

LOOK INSIDE YOU

SELF CARE

LOOK INSIDE YOU

LOOK INSIDE YOU

**A little more self-love
and a lot less of their love.
Self love is your super power,
it can move mountains.
/LS**

LOOK INSIDE YOU

Amazing things happen when
you learn to love yourself.
Your energy moves into
activation mode and
your spirit levels up.
Each day is a new opportunity
to move forward and encourage
your own potential.
Life gets so effortless because you hold so
much love and respect for yourself
that you apply it to those
people around you.
You are dynamic and aligning
and that's a beautiful thing.

/LS

LOOK INSIDE YOU

Girl, eat those cookies.
drink that bottle of wine.
Turn up the music
and dance all over the house.
Talk on the phone with
your friends all night.
Sleep all day.
Buy fresh flowers
for your room.
Write poetry.
Paint your toenails.
These are all acts of self care,
that you deserve any time you feel like it.
Revel in it.
Do it often.
Celebrate yourself.
Nourish your heart
Feed your soul.
Spend copious amounts of
time on yourself.
Because you are deserving,
don't let yourself forget that.

/LS

LOOK INSIDE YOU

No hate, but there are many
people I'm glad I'm not close to anymore.
Cutting them off is self-care.
Don't feel obliged to
feed unhealthy connections in your life.
Love yourself enough
to appreciate the sound of your feet
walking away from them.
You've grown.

/LS

LOOK INSIDE YOU

Isn't it funny how bothered people become
when you're unbothered?
Let them lose it.
Let them be pissed.
Respect yourself too much
to react and fall
into their toxic traps.
you are better than that.

/LS

LOOK INSIDE YOU

You owe it to yourself
to become all the
things you've dreamt of becoming.
So please, when things
seems like they're not moving,
don't abandon yourself.
Stay with yourself.

/LS

LOOK INSIDE YOU

It can be difficult to love yourself,
but it is more difficult
to *not* love yourself.
You have to love and embrace
who you are and celebrate your uniqueness.
Stop putting yourself down,
you have endless galaxies inside you.
Love all of you,
all the body parts you hate
looking at in the mirror,
your complex mind and your intricate soul,
because it is all you,
in one perfect package.
So start treating yourself
gentler and nurture you.
Bestow compassion on yourself.
Love yourself wholeheartedly,
otherwise no one else will.

/LS

LOOK INSIDE YOU

LOOK INSIDE YOU

HEARTBREAK

LOOK INSIDE YOU

I have learned enough
to never need
another lesson
in heartbreak again.

/LS

LOOK INSIDE YOU

You taught me all
the things about love
I didn't want to know.

/LS

LOOK INSIDE YOU

Sometimes I wish I
could merely switch
my feelings off and not have
to suffer this pain.
But I know I must acknowledge it
for it to to eventually have mercy on me.

/LS

LOOK INSIDE YOU

> Just because we didn't end up in the same wave doesn't mean we aren't part of the same ocean.
>
> /LS

LOOK INSIDE YOU

He was never mine,
and I knew this from the start.
But losing him
shattered my heart
into a thousand pieces.
I just wasn't ready to forget him.
And it wasn't the first broken heart I suffered.
But every single one
was gut wrenching nevertheless.
I wasn't ready to face the world alone,
and I don't think I ever will be.
That is my weakness.
I am my own worst enemy

/LS

LOOK INSIDE YOU

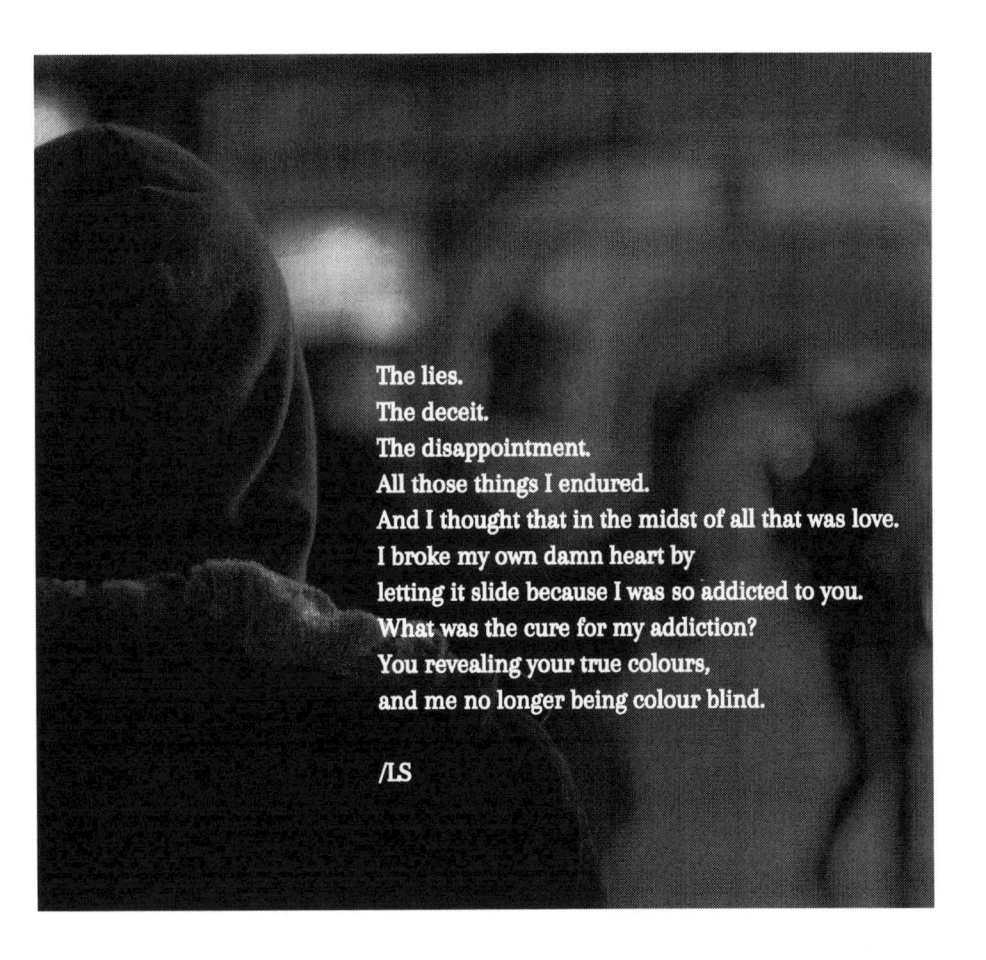

The lies.
The deceit.
The disappointment.
All those things I endured.
And I thought that in the midst of all that was love.
I broke my own damn heart by
letting it slide because I was so addicted to you.
What was the cure for my addiction?
You revealing your true colours,
and me no longer being colour blind.

/LS

LOOK INSIDE YOU

My heart wanted to be
yours so badly
that it asked for you
to break it
rather
than never
have it at all.

/LS

LOOK INSIDE YOU

And in that moment I felt
my voice quiver
and my heart almost stop.
I escaped with
every part of me suffering.
But all those parts
were telling me that
they were with me to
end this relationship.
They were tired of
being imprisoned.
The thought of the heartache
I must endure
almost makes me hesitate,
but I know it is for the best
as I walk towards my liberty
with my head held high.

/LS

LOOK INSIDE YOU

Missing someone's love brings a certain
type of pain.
A pain that spreads and persists.
A pain that tells you something
is missing.
When someone is no longer
in your life,
it feels as if they literally
took a part of us with them.
Their absence is like the loss
of a vital organ.
Usually the heart.

/LS

LOOK INSIDE YOU

LOOK INSIDE YOU

HEALING

LOOK INSIDE YOU

LOOK INSIDE YOU

I never thought I'd
move on or recover
from the collapse.
But I woke up this morning
and I realised it was your
birthday yesterday and
I'd actually forgotten.
And when I realised that,
I knew I was half way to healing.

/LS

LOOK INSIDE YOU

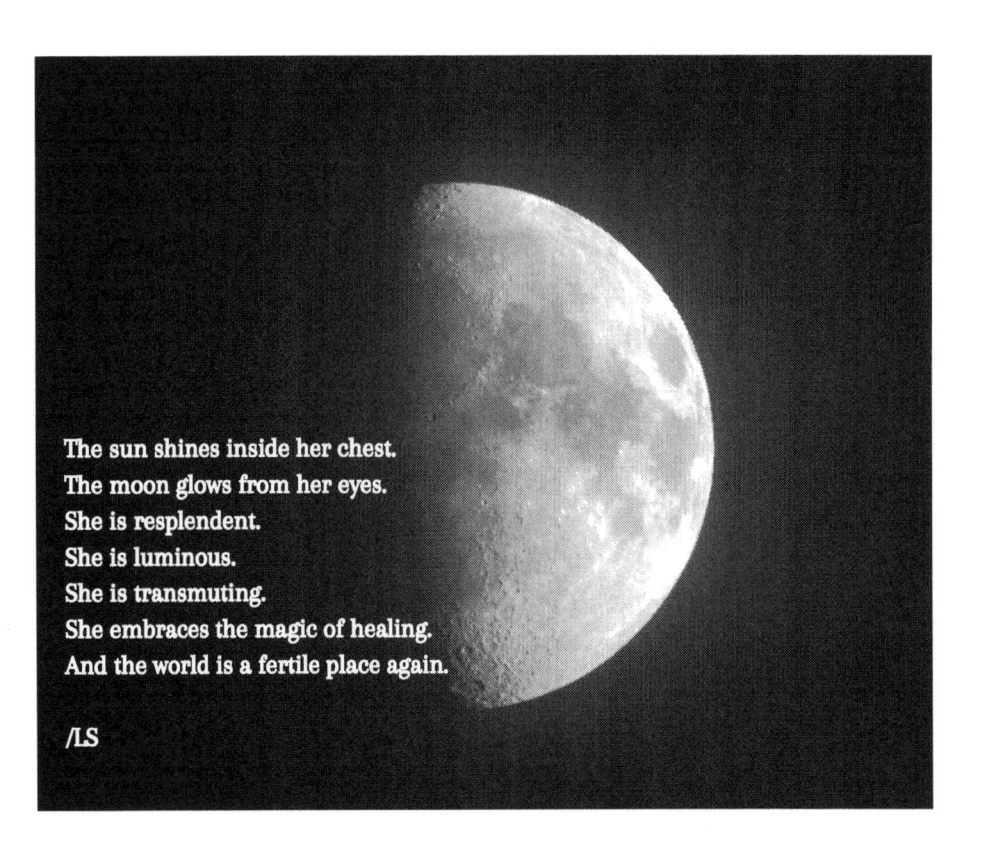

The sun shines inside her chest.
The moon glows from her eyes.
She is resplendent.
She is luminous.
She is transmuting.
She embraces the magic of healing.
And the world is a fertile place again.

/LS

LOOK INSIDE YOU

Be gentle and patient
with yourself.
The scars will resurface
every now and then.
Those wounds without
a doubt you will still feel.
But just as you broke,
so shall you heal.

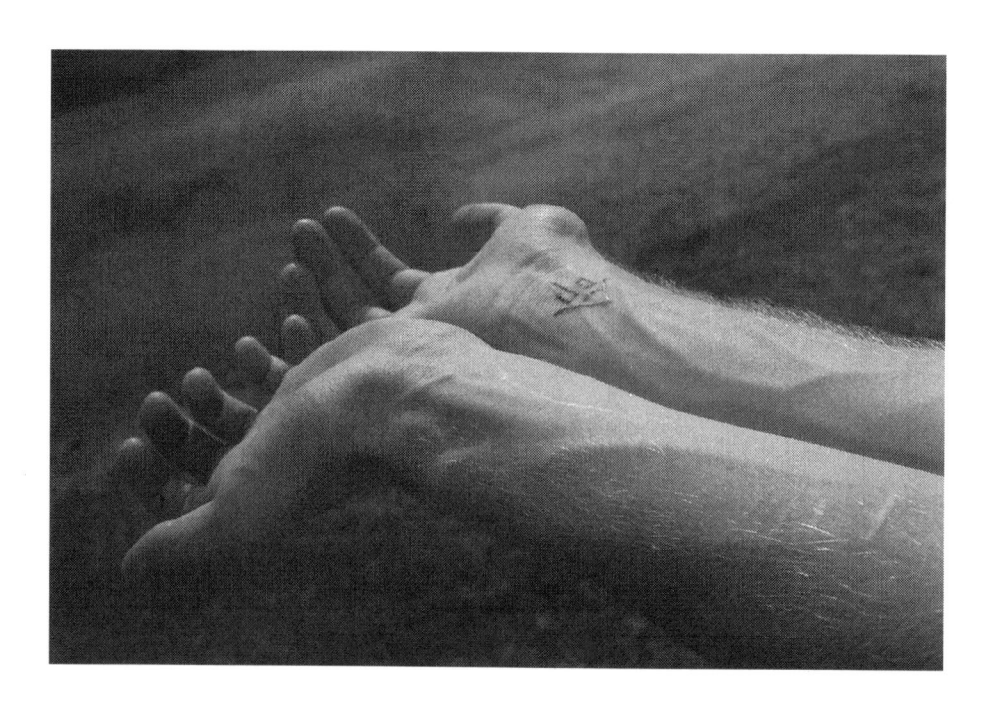

/LS

LOOK INSIDE YOU

The hardest thing I have learned
is that I can't force myself
to heal.
I just need to be there for
myself and it's as
simple as that.

/LS

LOOK INSIDE YOU

I discovered myself
while I was lost.
And somewhere in the
midst of a wrong turn
and a poor choice,
I came to the conclusion that
I needed to be found.
I cast off who I thought
I was supposed to be,
and I became all that I knew
I could be.
I've never looked back,
I'm not going that way anymore.

/LS

LOOK INSIDE YOU

I shouldn't need to apologise
for making choices,
or letting go of things
for the sake of
saving my sanity.
Because I'll always choose me.
For that I'll never be sorry.

/LS

LOOK INSIDE YOU

You have to do the work.
You have to be at peace
with what you've been through,
and what you've done.
Start looking ahead at where
you see yourself going.
The person you want to become
is on the other side of that.
Stop being triggered.
Rise above things
that you reacted to before,
and you will heal your fractured heart.
You will transform your life.

/LS

LOOK INSIDE YOU

Sometimes you have to release
the life you thought you wanted
so that you can openly embrace
the one that is waiting
for you.
Letting go is tough,
but be prepared to await
a better future.
The one you have been
keeping at arms length.
Let today be the beginning
of all that.
You have the world at your feet
and the stars in your eyes.

/LS

LOOK INSIDE YOU

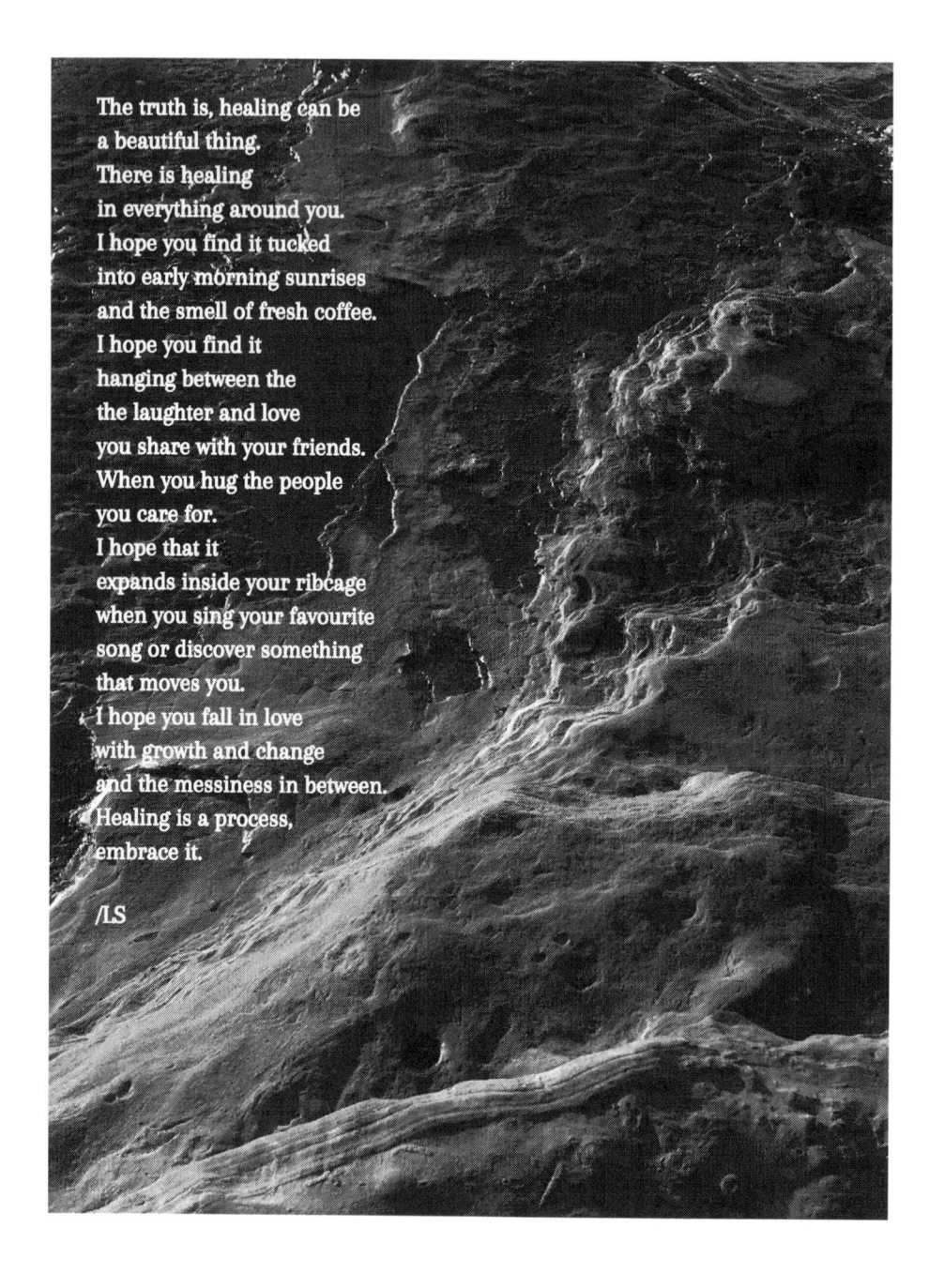

The truth is, healing can be
a beautiful thing.
There is healing
in everything around you.
I hope you find it tucked
into early morning sunrises
and the smell of fresh coffee.
I hope you find it
hanging between the
the laughter and love
you share with your friends.
When you hug the people
you care for.
I hope that it
expands inside your ribcage
when you sing your favourite
song or discover something
that moves you.
I hope you fall in love
with growth and change
and the messiness in between.
Healing is a process,
embrace it.

/LS

LOOK INSIDE YOU

Healing doesn't mean you'll
never get triggered again,
or that you're miraculously
going to arrive at a place
free of pain and suffering.
Healing is a subdued homecoming.
It's about settling peacefully
into the realness of who you are.
Not being that fragmented
and broken person you've become.
But realising you are
worthy of love and you
are human, even in pieces.

/LS

LOOK INSIDE YOU

Everyone says falling in love is
like a fairytale,
but hesitate
to tell you the reality
of what it's really like.
When you fall,
no one is there to catch you.
So you're left lying in the
dust with your heart
in pieces on the floor.
So you see, falling in love
is far from a fairytale.
the fall breaks more
than just your bones.

/LS

LOOK INSIDE YOU

LOOK INSIDE YOU

JOY

LOOK INSIDE YOU

LOOK INSIDE YOU

The simplest things bring the
most joy.
And only the wise can
truly see it.

/LS

LOOK INSIDE YOU

By giving joy to others
you cultivate joy.
Let yourself experience
the fulfilment you obtain
from bestowing joy
upon the world.

/LS

LOOK INSIDE YOU

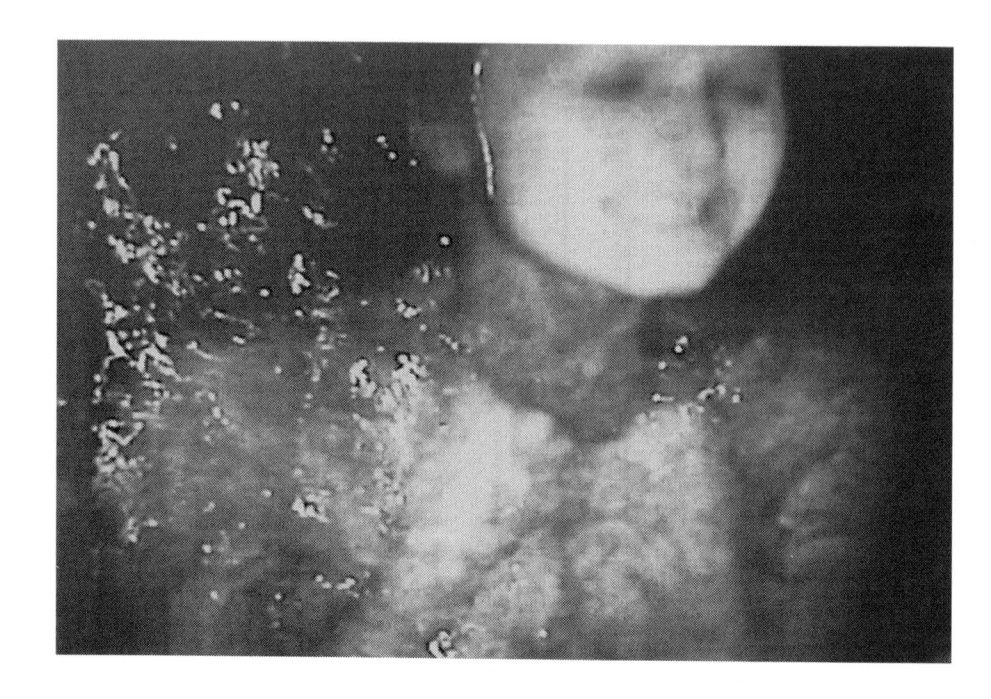

If tears of joy,
Tears of love,
Tears of happiness,
Tears of euphoria,
Have not yet graced
your cheeks,
You have not
truly lived.

/LS

LOOK INSIDE YOU

It was cold outside
but we didn't care
about any of that.
We wrapped ourselves
around each other
like a blanket.
We made our own fire.
These humble moments of sheer
delight will never leave me.

/LS

LOOK INSIDE YOU

And as a delicious
river of joyous tears
make their way
down my cheeks,
they drip from
my chin into a
pool of appreciation on the ground.
An offering to the Gods
for all the good fortune
that I have been bestowed.

/LS

LOOK INSIDE YOU

There are beautiful moments
I wish I could take you to.
Emotions I wish I could
make you experience.
I want to make you feel
rapture,
delight,
pleasure,
bliss,
exhilaration,
gladness,
joyfulness.
My love could be
the thing to fill
the void.
Let me make you whole again.

/LS

LOOK INSIDE YOU

Never willingly go in search of happiness,
go in search of life.
And life will yield
the happiness you seek.
It's really that simple.

/LS

LOOK INSIDE YOU

A smile a day
keeps the demons away.
When you etch a smile
on your face,
you carve joy
in every place.

/LS

LOOK INSIDE YOU

Joy is that sublime moment
when you begin
to feel a little
bit closer to
all that is glorious.

/LS

LOOK INSIDE YOU

Choose joy in the pauses.
Choose to live in the present
moment with pure,
unbridled faith that
never lets go,.
It reminds you
that things are still
working their way out.
Things will take time
to come about,
but you can still
choose joy while
you wait it out.

/LS

LOOK INSIDE YOU

You carry within you
all the ingredients
to bake yourself
the most sublime
joyful existence.
Mix, fold and whip them together
and put a cherry on the top.

/LS

LOOK INSIDE YOU

Venus gazed upon the moon,
jealous of it's luminous beauty,
wishing she could shine
as brilliantly.
But the moon told her
not to envy him,
for she was the most
beautiful star in the sky.
The one humans gazed up
at with adoring eyes.
She smiled and gracefully
bowed her head,
thanking the moon.
For she had no idea
of her own magnificence.
And they graciously danced to
the symphony of the stars
adored by all from near and far.

/LS

LOOK INSIDE YOU

LOOK INSIDE YOU

Thank you for reading this book. I hope you
have enjoyed it and that you have a look at my
other collections which are listed at the front of
the book.

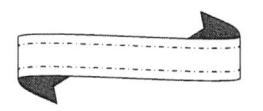

Printed in Poland
by Amazon Fulfillment
Poland Sp. z o.o., Wrocław